D1463340

Healthy
Eating

Fruits and
Vegetables

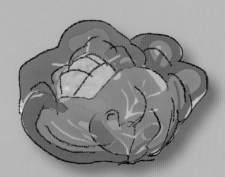

Susan Martineau
and Hel James

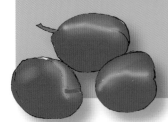

A+
Smart Apple Media

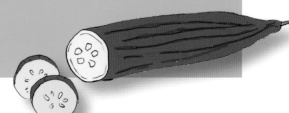

Published by Smart Apple Media
2140 Howard Drive West, North Mankato, MN 56003

Designed and illustrated by Helen James
Edited by Jinny Johnson

Photographs: 11 Owaki-Kulla/Corbis; 12-13 Patrick Johns/Corbis; 14 Helen James; 15 Michael Pole/Corbis;
16 Douglas Peebles/Corbis; 17 Peter Turnley/Corbis; 19 Michael Boys/Corbis; 21 Steve Terrill/Corbis; 23 Eric
Crichton/Corbis; 24 Richard Morrell/Corbis; 26 Daniel Boschung/Zefa/Corbis; 29 PhotoCuisine/Corbis:
Front cover: Ed Young/Corbis

Printed in Thailand

Library of Congress Catalog-in-Publication Data
Martineau, Susan.
Healthy eating. Fruits and vegetables / by Susan Martineau
p. cm.
Includes index.
ISBN-13: 978-1-58340-896-4
1. Fruits—Juvenile literature. 2. Vegetables—Juvenile literature. I. Title. II. Title: Fruits and vegetables.

TX397.M285 2006
641.3'4—dc22   2006009396

First Edition

9 8 7 6 5 4 3 2 1

Contents

Food for health

Our bodies are like amazing machines.
Just like machines, we need the right
kind of fuel to give us energy and
to keep us working properly.

If we don't eat the kind of food we need to keep us healthy, we may become ill or feel tired and grumpy. Our bodies do not like it if we eat too much of one kind of food, like cakes or chips.

We need a balanced diet. That means eating different kinds of good food in the right amounts.

You'll be surprised at how much there is to know about where our food comes from and why some kinds of food are better for us than others. Finding out about food is great fun and very tasty!

What's so good about fruit and vegetables?

Eating at least five different fruits and vegetables every day helps you stay healthy.

They're full of vitamins and minerals.

A balanced meal!

The good things, or **nutrients**, that our bodies need come from different kinds of food. Let's look at what your plate should have on it. It all looks delicious!

Rice, bread, and pasta

These foods contain **carbohydrates** and they give us energy. About a third of our food should come from this group.

Fruits and vegetables

Rice, bread, and pasta

Bread, cheese, and salad give you carbohydrates, protein, vitamins, and minerals.

Fruits and vegetables

These are full of great **vitamins**, **minerals**, and **fiber**. They help keep you healthy. About a third of our food should come from this group.

Milk, yogurt, and cheese

These dairy foods give us protein and **calcium** to make strong bones and teeth.

Meat, fish, and eggs

Protein from these helps your body grow and repair itself. They are body-building foods. We should eat some every day.

Sugar and fats

We only need small amounts of these. Too much can be bad for our teeth and make us overweight.

Milk, yogurt, and cheese

Sugar and fats

Meat, fish, and eggs

Water

We need to drink at least six glasses of water every day.

Vital vitamins and magic minerals

Fruits and vegetables give us many wonderful vitamins and minerals. These help us grow and stay healthy. Fruits and vegetables also give us fiber. Fiber keeps our **digestive system** working properly.

High five!

Try to eat five portions of fruit and vegetables every day. Choose different ones so you have a great balance of vitamins and minerals. There are many different kinds of delicious fruits and vegetables, so it's easy to eat lots of them!

Super-charged menu

Breakfast

Have some fresh fruit on your cereal.

Super-charged menu

Lunch

Put some salad in your lunchbox!

You can get fresh, frozen, or canned vegetables.

Super-charged menu

Dinner

Have some carrots and broccoli with your evening meal.

Fantastic fruits

Fruits grow on trees, bushes, and plants. All flowering plants have seeds. The fleshy fruit is what forms around the seeds to protect them. How many different kinds of fruits can you think of? Do they have lots of little seeds or one big one, called a stone?

Oranges and lemons

Oranges, lemons, and limes are called **citrus fruits**. Other citrus fruits are satsumas, mandarins, clementines, and grapefruit. They all grow on trees. The seeds inside them are the seeds of the trees.

Lemon

Orange

Lime

Freshly squeezed fruit juice is packed with vitamins.

Grapefruit

Oranges are picked and put into big tubs. Then they go to a packing house to be checked, washed, and labeled.

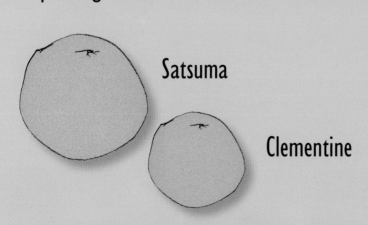

Satsuma

Clementine

Citrus fruits are full of **Vitamin C**. This helps keep the body strong to fight off illness.

Apples, pears, and plums

Apples and pears are hard fruits with small seeds inside them. Plums have just one large stone in the middle. Other fruits with one big stone are nectarines, peaches, apricots, and cherries. All these fruits grow on trees.

Snack on some delicious cherries but watch out for the stones!

Pears

Plums

12

Apples have to be picked by hand because machines would bruise them. They are washed and then stored in cold buildings to keep them fresh.

Make a juicy fruit salad with all of your favorite fruits.

When you eat one of these delicious fruits, you are giving your body many different nutrients as well as fiber. Peaches, nectarines, and apricots have lots of **Vitamin A** in them. Vitamin A is good for your eyes.

Berries and grapes

Strawberries, raspberries, blueberries, and blackberries are all loaded with Vitamin C. Berries are delicious eaten just as they are. They can also be mixed into yogurts or cooked to make jam.

Grapes grow in big bunches on long, trailing plants called **vines**. You can get green or red grapes. Some grapes are dried to make raisins.

Strawberries

Raspberries

Blueberries

Blackberries

Cut a kiwi in half and scoop out the sweet green flesh and seeds. This gives you all of the Vitamin C your body needs for a day.

A kiwi fruit looks like a brown furry egg. It also grows on a plant like a vine.

Find out if there is a farm near you where you can pick your own berries. How about making some jam?

Black currants

Tropical fruits

Bananas, pineapples, and mangoes grow in tropical countries. It is hot and sunny all year there, with lots of rain, so it is perfect for growing these fruits. Try to find out about other tropical fruits, such as papayas and lychees. See how many of them you can find in your local stores.

Mangoes grow on trees and have a large, flat stone inside their sweet, orange flesh. A ripe mango is a delicious treat full of Vitamins C and A.

Bananas grow on very large plants that look like trees. Many bunches, or hands, of bananas grow on the plant. They are picked when they are still green.

The bananas are checked and labeled before being packed into boxes. Then the bananas are carried by ships to different parts of the world. They are kept in big refrigerators to keep them fresh.

How many fruits can you find in my hat?

17

Vegetables galore

A vegetable is any part of a plant that can be eaten. It can be the leaves, stalks, buds, or roots of a plant. There are lots of delicious vegetables to choose. You could ask all of your friends to name their favorite one to find out which one is the most popular!

Eat your greens!

Green vegetables are very good for you. They have many kinds of great nutrients and fiber in them.

Cauliflower is in the same vegetable family as broccoli and cabbage.

Broccoli is the flower bud of a plant.

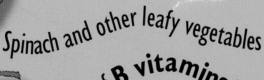

Spinach and other leafy vegetables contain lots of **B vitamins** to keep us healthy.

Fruit vegetables

Some vegetables are called fruit vegetables.
They have juicy flesh and come in many kinds
of vitamin-packed shapes, sizes, and colors.

Tomatoes, peppers, and eggplants grow on small
bushes. In cooler countries, farmers grow them in
large glass houses called greenhouses.

Avocados grow on trees and look like pears.
They are full of vitamins and minerals.

Cucumbers, squash, zucchini, and pumpkins
are all in the same vegetable family. They grow
on trailing bushes or vines.

Avocado

Eggplants and
peppers

They're not
cherries—
they're cherry
tomatoes!

Cucumber

Tomatoes are tasty
little packages of
Vitamin C.

Pumpkins can be made into a golden soup.

Pods and seeds

French beans, runner beans, and mangetout (or snow peas) are all pods. They grow on climbing plants. We can cook and eat the whole pod including the little beans or peas inside them.

Peas grow inside pods. It's fun to take the peas out of their pods, but in factories, there is a special machine called a viner to do this.

Frozen peas

Peas and other vegetables are often frozen before being sold in the shops. They are frozen as soon as they are picked so that they keep all of their good vitamins inside them.

Corn on the cob

Sweet corn is the seeds of a grass plant. We can eat the seeds, or kernels, straight off the cob they grow on.

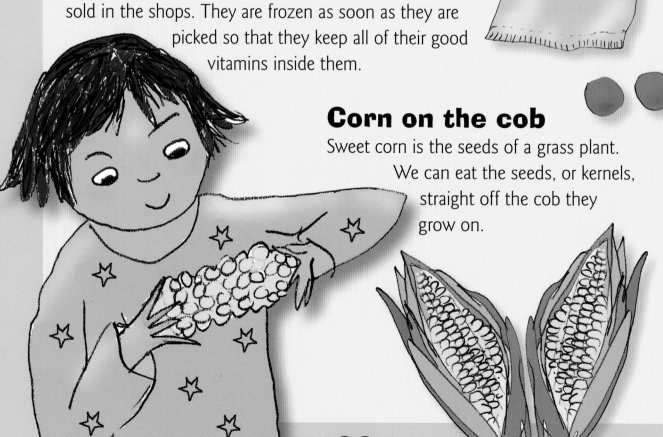

It's easy to grow your own runner beans.

Did you know that popcorn is made out of corn kernels?

Pea pod and peas

Vegetables
under the ground

Potatoes, carrots, beets, and parsnips are all vegetables that grow under the ground. They are called root vegetables. They give us lots of vitamins and fiber. Carrots are full of Vitamin A.

Potatoes are dug up by machines. The farmer checks through them and takes out any bad ones.

Beets

Parsnips

Carrots

What about organic vegetables?

Vegetable growers often use special **chemicals** to kill bugs and weeds and make the vegetables grow better. Some people think these chemicals are bad for us and they harm the **environment**. **Organic** vegetables are grown without using chemicals.

Fries?

Baked potato?

Potatoes can be boiled, mashed, baked, or made into chips and fries. Chips and fries are cooked in lots of fat so they are not the healthiest way to eat potatoes.

A bowl of salad

You can make a salad with many kinds of lettuce leaves. You can also use baby spinach leaves or watercress. They taste quite strong so it is nice to mix them with other leaves too.

Pots of herbs

Herbs add a nice taste to all kinds of meals. You could grow your own in pots on a windowsill.

Basil smells wonderful and is used to make a delicious sauce called pesto that tastes great on pasta.

Mint is good with lamb dishes or with vegetables like potatoes or peas.

Curly parsley

Parsley can be sprinkled on top of dishes or added to soups and stews.

Flat-leaf parsley

Have a salad with your supper or snack on a bowl of raw vegetables. Try carrot sticks, radishes, and celery. They are delicious in your lunchbox, too.

Loads of lentils

Lentils, chickpeas, and different kinds of beans are the dried seeds of bean and pea plants. These dried seeds are called pulses. They keep for months and are great for making soups, curries, and stews.

Pulses are full of protein and so they are good for vegetarians who do not get protein from meat. They also contain iron and fiber. Soy beans can be made into bean curd, or **tofu**.

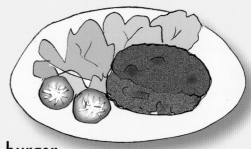

Veggie burger

Beans on toast

Chilli con carne

Bring on the beans!

Canned baked beans are very good for you. They are made from dried haricot beans and tomato sauce. Try to find the ones with "low sugar" and "low salt" on the label.

Chickpea stew

Red lentils

Split peas

Borlotti beans

Cannellini beans

Chickpeas

Kidney beans

Puy lentils

Soy beans

Corn

Words to remember

B vitamins   B vitamins help turn our food into energy and keep our muscles, skin and blood healthy. B Vitamins have special names like folate, niacin and thiamin. If you see these on a label you know the food has B Vitamins in it. Green leafy vegetables contain folate.

calcium   A mineral which helps build healthy bones and teeth. Spinach and broccoli have calcium in them.

carbohydrates   Starches and sugars in food that give us energy. Carbohydrate foods are rice, pasta, bread, and potatoes. Bananas have carbohydrates in them, so they give us lots of energy, too.

chemicals   Chemicals are substances that can be used for all sorts of things. Some, called pesticides, are used to kill weeds and bugs in fields.

citrus fruits   Fruits like oranges, lemons, limes, and grapefruit. They have a thick skin and juicy flesh.

digestive system   The parts of your body where your food gets broken down and turned into energy and nutrients.

environment   The world around us.

fiber   Fiber is found in plant foods like grains and vegetables. It helps our insides work properly.

iron   A mineral in food that we need to keep our blood healthy.

minerals   Nutrients in food that help our bodies work properly. Calcium and iron are minerals.

nutrients   Parts of food that your body needs to make energy, to grow healthily, and to repair itself.

organic   Organic fruits and vegetables are grown without using chemicals.

protein   Body-building food that makes our bodies grow well and stay healthy.

tofu   This is also called bean curd. It is a cheese-like food made out of soy beans.

vines   Long, trailing plants. Grapes and kiwi fruit grow on vines.

vitamin A   This vitamin is in most dark green or yellow fruits and vegetables. It helps us stay healthy and it is especially good for our eyes.

vitamin C   Keeps our gums and teeth healthy, mends cuts and bruises, and makes us strong to fight off infection and illness. Our bodies cannot store Vitamin C so we need some every day.

vitamins   Nutrients in food that help our bodies work properly.

Index

Web sites

Learn which foods make a healthy heart.
http://www.healthyfridge.org/

Test your nutritional knowledge with quizzes, dietary guidelines, and a glossary of terms.
http://www.exhibits.pacsci.org/nutrition/

Find out how to have a healthy diet without eating meat.
http://www.vrg.org/family/kidsindex.htm

Get the facts about fast food restaurants and tips for making healthy choices.
http://library.thinkquest.org/4485/

Take the 5-a-day challenge and learn about fruits and vegetables with puzzles, music, and games.
http://www.dole5aday.com/

Discover ten tips for a healthy lifestyle.
http://www.fitness.gov/10tips.htm